Pet Paradise

Dandy Ahuruonye

Published by Dandy Ahuruonye, 2024.

PET PARADISE

First edition. January 29, 2024.

ISBN: 979-8224337378

Written by Dandy Ahuruonye.

Also by Dandy Ahuruonye

In loving remembrance of Mr Mezie Reward Friday Ahuruonye, who left this world too soon. *Meme*, you live on in our minds....! ◈

PET PARADISE

DANDY AHAOMA AHURUONYE

The Whispering Poet

1

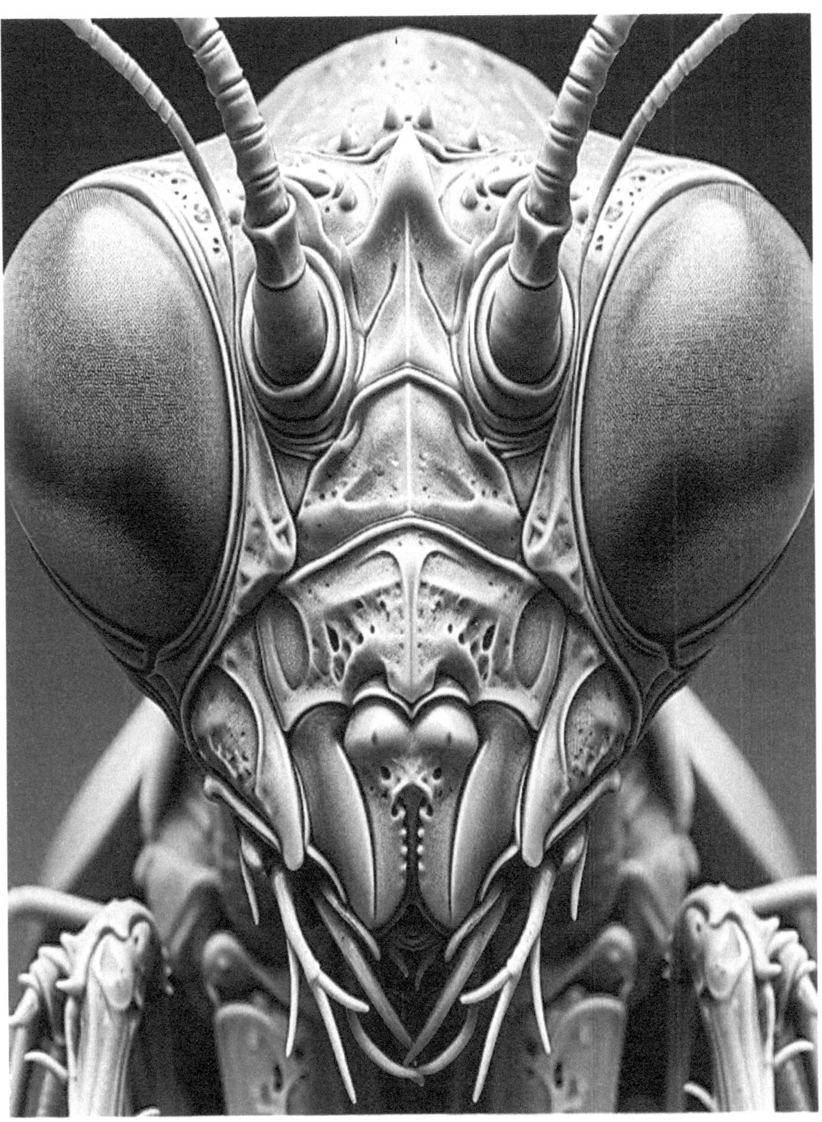

APPRECIATION

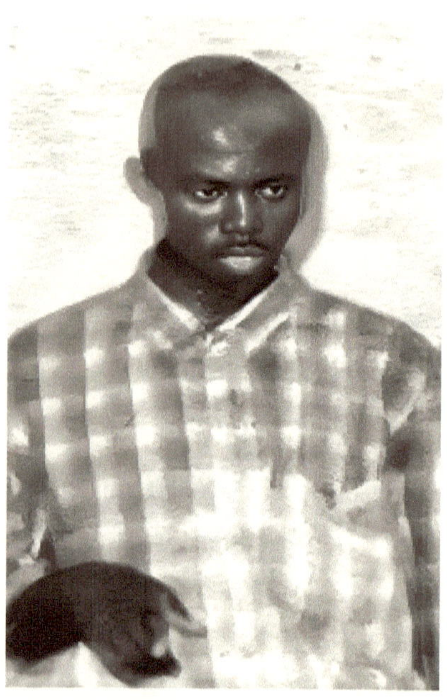

In loving remembrance of Mr Mezie Reward Friday Ahuruonye, who left this life too soon. *Meme*, you live on in our minds....! ◈

DANDY AHAOMA AHURUONYE

PET PARADISE

Here are two important lessons for you, beloved little ones: ◈
It is more beneficial when you focus on the sound instead of the echo.
Know your destination because people always give way to those who know where they're going.

CREDITS

With digital illustrations by De Juvenyles
dandyahuruonyebooks.com
Original life stories from the Whispering Poet

INTRODUCTION

What if you could see your pets again, even after they die? If you could hug them, play with them, and love them forever, what would you be willing to give to make that happen? If there was a place where your pets could live happily, healthily, and peacefully with you and other animals, would you agree to go there? Well, that's what Didi, a clever engineer, dreamed of when she lost her beloved dog. She had a brilliant idea: to use a powerful computer program to resurrect dead pets and return them to life. She called her pet return to life program Pet Paradise. Didi created an AI supercomputer called Groccolli, a smart robot that could run and maintain the pet paradise. She gave him a mission: to bring back to life as many pets and animals as possible and to make them happy and healthy. Groccolli did his best, and he brought back to life many creatures, including monarch butterflies and praying mantises. The intelligent robot taught them how to talk, and he made them friends and families, as well as a home and a garden. However, Pet Paradise was not perfect. There were still problems that the pets and animals had to face, like blood-sucking mosquitoes, pollution, fear, and even death. Didi and Groccolli wanted to make Pet Paradise a proper paradise, where no pet or animal would ever get sick, grow old, or die. They wanted it to be a place of happiness, peace, and love for everyone, forever. Consequently, they worked on a new and improved program, a program that would make the place a real paradise, a program that would solve all the problems and a program that would make everyone happy, healthy, and immortal. They called it The Real Pet Paradise.

The engineer and Groccolli hoped to someday take the pets and animals to this better environment; where no one would ever have to worry about anything again, never again had to say goodbye. They had everything they ever wanted, and more. They had a true paradise, and they had Didi and Groccolli. But there was one more thing they needed, one more thing that would make their paradise complete. Yes, they needed humans, humans who would adopt them, love them, and care for them; humans who would be their friends, their families, their companions. That's where you come in. Could you be one of those humans? Could you adopt one of those pets or animals? You can be their friend, their family, and their companion.

All you have to do is read this book and find out how. This book will tell you the amazing story of Didi, Groccolli, and the pets and animals of Pet Paradise. It will show you the wonders of both Pet Paradise and The Real Pet Paradise. This book will inspire you to use your imagination and your dreams and to create your own happiness and love. It will make you think, and it will make you better. Pet Paradise is waiting for you; don't miss this chance to discover the mystery, the adventure and the fun, the beauty and the joy of Pet Paradise. Seize this chance to meet the amazing characters, the clever engineer, the smart robot, the monarch butterflies, the mantises, and many more; those who made Pet Paradise a dream come true. Don't miss this chance to be part of the story.

By reading on, you too could enter Pet Paradise with these adorable little friends!

A PARADE OF THE TAMED

To our young readers, ◈
    Here is a poem from the pets; please note that this is simply a creative work of fiction and not intended to cause any harm or offence to anyone or any pet:

A dog, a cat, a hamster too
They all had collars, shiny and new
They were at Pet Paradise, a place so grand
Where they could play and run on the sand
Yes, pets are cool, they have it all
They go to Paradise when they fall asleep
But others want to join, they feel left out
They queue up for humans, they shout and pout
They show off their talents, to make a bargain
Each says to the watching humans, "Let me in!"
They offer their skills, and try to impress
They say, "We'll be loyal, if just say yes!"
The cow argues, "I'm a milk factory
I'll also trim your lawn, for no fee"
A horse says, "I'm in transport service
I'll also race for you, I'm very fast"
A pig says, "I'm a truffle finder
I'll also crack you up, I'm a joker"
A chicken says, "I'm an egg maker
I'll also wake you up, I'm a rooster"
A fish utters, "I'm a tank decorator
I'll also sing for you, I'm a crooner"
A bird says, "I'm a sky explorer
I'll also talk to you, I'm a parrot"
An ant says, "I'm a hard worker

I'll teach you teamwork, I'm a leader"
A bee says, "I'm a honey machine
I'll boost your garden, I'm a pollinator"
A spider speaks, "I'm a web designer
I'll also catch the bugs; I'm a hunter"
A worm says, "I'm a soil engineer
I'll recycle your waste, the digester"
So stunned by creatures skilled with gifts
The humans took them in with charms
To scan them with Groccolli that code
They put collars on them, with tags and names
"Welcomed pets; we'll love you with hugs"
The pets so glad, they thanked them with joy
"From here to bliss, with friends we come
To sing together, as we board the portal
We're your pets; you're our pals, forever!"

PART TWO

Pets are lucky, they've got our badge
They go to Paradise, when they upload
But others want to join, they have no key
They queue up for humans, they send an API
They show their features, they make a pitch
They say to humans, "Please click and switch"
They offer their functions, they try to debug
They say, "We'll be useful, just plug and unplug"
A cow says, "I'm a milk generator
I'll also be your grass terminator"
A horse says, "I'm a transport module
I'll also be your race gateway"
A pig says, "I'm a virus detector
I'll also be your humour injector"
A chicken says, "I'm an egg creator
I'll also be your alarm activator"
A fish says, "I'm a tank beautifier
I'll also be your music amplifier"
A bird says, "I'm a sky scanner
I'll also be your voice planner"
An ant says, "I'm a hard driver
I'll also be your teamwork printer"
A bee says, "I'm a honey producer
I'll also be your garden engineer"
A spider says, "I'm a web designer
I'll also be your bug remover"
A worm says, "I'm a soil enricher
I'll also be your waste bin recycler"
The humans impressed by creatures so skilled
Agreed to X-ray all with the Groccolli scanner
They give them collars and pets they became
They'll code and love them; they're family anew
Pets so ecstatic, they thank the humans dearly
To upload to Paradise, with allies plugged
They sing binary songs, as they hop on the USB
"We're your pets; you're our bosses, forever!"

1: THE MONARCH BUTTERFLY

Imagine a sea of creatures in a fluttering parade of orange and black soaring across the sky in a magnificent spectacle. This is the monarch butterfly, a wonder of nature that travels thousands of kilometres every year, from the inhospitable lands of North America to the warm forests of Mexico. Along the way, they face many perils and hardships, such as storms, predators, hunger, and pollution. But they never lose hope or direction, guided by a mysterious force that scientists call Groccolli; the android that makes dreams come true. They find a partner and lay their eggs on special plants called milkweed, where their babies will grow and feed. The adult butterflies then die peacefully, knowing that they have passed on their legacy to the coming generation. ◇

Meet Orion and Ophelia, a beautiful pair of monarch butterflies who live in a meadow full of flowers and insects. The couple is happy and content with their life, but they also have a dream. They want to travel to the warm forests of Mexico, where their ancestors have gone for generations. They know that this journey will be long and dangerous, and they will not survive after laying their eggs. However, they also know that this is their purpose, and their children will carry on with their legacy. A mysterious force, which scientists call Groccolli, guides them.

Groccolli is the android that makes their dreams come true.

One day, as they were resting on a sunflower, they talked about their dream.

"Ophelia, my love, you know how much I adore you, right?" Orion said, looking into her eyes.

"Of course, Orion, you are the best thing that ever happened to me," Ophelia replied, smiling.

"Then you also know that I want to make you happy and give you everything you deserve," Orion continued.

"Yes, I know that. And I feel the same way about you."

"Then, Ophelia, my darling, would you travel with me to Mexico?" Orion asked, holding her wings.

"Oh, darling, I don't know. I'm scared. It's so far and so dangerous. What if we don't make it? What if we get lost or eaten or hurt?" She said, trembling.

"My angel, don't be afraid. You and I can do this. We have to do this. It's our destiny. It's what our ancestors did, and what our children will do, and it makes us part of a bigger story, a story of courage and hope. We are not alone; you've got me and I've got you, and besides, we have Groccolli; the android that makes dreams come true. He will help us find our way and protect us from harm. He will also watch over our eggs and make sure they hatch and grow. You and I will live on through them, and they will remember us," Orion told her in a comforting tone.

"Orion, my hero, you are so brave. A part of me wants to believe you, I really do, but I'm still scared. I love you so much, and I don't want to lose you. I don't want to die," Ophelia said, but she was now crying.

"My dearest Ophelia, nothing in this world can surpass my love for you. Nor do I wish to part with you ever. Yet we must accept the reality. Our existence is not eternal. Our destiny is to bestow life upon our offspring and allow them to soar freely. This is the most precious present we can offer them, and the highest privilege we can enjoy. Naturally, this act of creation will also be our demise, but we shall depart with joy, aware that we accomplished our mission, and that we brought happiness to each other. Perishing in unison, embracing each other's wings, and gazing at the heavens would be a sublime experience. We shall perish, but we shall not vanish. We shall endure in our children's souls and Groccolli's recollection. He will narrate our tale to them, and they will pass it on to their descendants, and so forth. We shall be part of a splendid and infinite circle of life," Orion said, wiping her tears.

"My beloved Orion, you speak the truth. You always do. You have persuaded me. I shall accompany you to Mexico. I shall confront the perils and the hardships. I shall pursue our fate. I shall bestow life upon our offspring and allow them to soar freely. I shall perish with you, but I shall perish joyfully. I shall endure in our children's souls and in Groccolli's recollection. We shall be part of a splendid and infinite circle of life," Ophelia said with a little smile on her face. They kissed and cuddled, feeling overjoyed.

The following day, when the sun was radiant and the wind was breezy, Orion and Ophelia resolved to depart. The couple wished to commence their voyage on a luminous and merry note and to relish their last days together. Orion and Ophelia devoted their time to flying, frolicking, and discovering the meadow, cherishing every instant. They also searched for a suitable spot to deposit their eggs, somewhere secure and concealed from foes. They eventually discovered an ideal location: a cluster of milkweed plants beside a stream, where they could behold the water and the sky. Orion and Ophelia fashioned a snug nest among the foliage and readied themselves for their momentous day. When the day arrived, they were prepared. They smooched and cuddled, and expressed to each other how much they adored each other. Then, they placed their eggs on the lower side of the leaves and enveloped them with some silk. The pair afterwards gazed at each other and expressed their gratitude for their present. ◈

"Ophelia, my angel, you have given me the most precious gift of all: our children. I will always love you, and I will always remember you," Orion told her, with tears in his eyes.

"Orion, my hero, you have made me the happiest butterfly in the world. My affection for you is everlasting, and my presence with you is constant."

Orion and Ophelia flew away, carried by the wind and the sun. They joined a massive flock of monarch butterflies, all migrating to Mexico. They flew for days and nights, over mountains, rivers, forests, and fields. Along the way, they faced many challenges, such as storms, predators, and pollution. But they never lost hope or direction, guided by Groccolli, an android that helps dreams come true. Eventually, the couple reached their destination: the warm and lush forests of Mexico, where they were surrounded by millions of other monarch butterflies, hanging from the trees like living decorations. Orion and Ophelia felt a sense of awe and wonder, as well as a sense of belonging and fulfilment. They had succeeded in their journey. Orion and Ophelia found a place to rest among the millions of butterflies and looked at each other, smiling. They had both achieved their goal of bringing happiness to each other. They closed their eyes and died, feeling happy and satisfied. Orion and Ophelia had given their lives for their offspring, who would continue their legacy.

This is the end of the first part of the story of Orion and Ophelia, the monarch butterfly couple who left their original home in North America and headed towards the warm forests of Mexico. What will happen to their eggs? Will they hatch and survive, find their own mates and have their own families? Will they ever learn about their parents and their sacrifice? Is there a chance that the young butterflies would one day encounter Groccolli? Read on to find out! ◈

2: THE EPIC MIGRATION

Behold, the finale of the larger-than-life tale of Orion and Ophelia, the valiant monarch butterflies who journeyed to Mexico and sacrificed their lives for their offspring. Groccolli, the android who grants wishes, aided them. This is also the tale of their progeny, who matured in the spring and soared back to North America. They discovered their own sustenance, their own abode, their companions, and their descendants. They learned about their parents' affection and devotion, and they encountered Groccolli, who revealed to them a secret. He uttered that they could reunite with their parents if they could find a way to go to Pet Paradise, a realm where deceased pets are brought back to life to live blissfully again. But to enter there, they had to transform into pets themselves. They had to locate a human who would adopt them before Groccolli could escort them to Pet Paradise. This is the story of their escapade, bravery, and aspiration.

The eggs that Orion and Ophelia deposited on the milkweed plants emerged as minuscule caterpillars. They devoured the foliage and expanded larger and larger, altered their skin repeatedly, and then fabricated a shell around themselves, termed a chrysalis. Within the chrysalis, they metamorphosed again and emerged as butterflies with signature orange and black wings. Their novel bodies astonished the butterflies, and so did the world surrounding them. Gazing at the flowers, the insects, the water, and the sky, the younglings marvelled at the beauty of creation. The tiny butterflies felt the warmth of the sun, the caress of the wind, and the freshness of the rain, smelled the fragrance of the nectar, the pollen, and the earth and listened to the songs of the birds, the buzz of the bees, and the croak of the frogs. They relished the sweetness, the bitterness, and the saltiness, and were overjoyed because of all the excitement. Their names were Manny and Mandy.

Manny and Mandy encountered other butterflies who had emerged in the spring and befriended them and together they frolicked and discovered their new environment. Manny and Mandy swiftly learned how to soar, how to locate nourishment, how to elude predators, and how to converse. They also acquired knowledge about their ancestry, their traditions, and their fate. Manny and Mandy were moved after discovering that their parents had journeyed far and confronted every sort of peril, to attain the balmy woodlands of Mexico where they had originated. These offspring discovered that their parents had perished there, after depositing their eggs on the milkweed plants, and that they had cherished them immensely, and had bestowed them the boon of existence. Discovering all this made them both sorrowful and dignified and made them comprehend how much their parents had accomplished for them and how much they were indebted to them. Manny and Mandy experienced a bond with their parents, Orion and Ophelia, and a longing to respect them. The youngsters resolved to pursue their parents' trail and to soar from Mexico back to North America, where they could behold the spot where their forebears had rested. Manny and Mandy also aspired to meet Groccolli, the android who fulfils dreams, and to express their gratitude for his assistance and direction. They prepared for their voyage, procuring food and water, and socialising with other butterflies who were also going on the journey. They awaited the opportune moment, when the sun was radiant and the wind was gentle, and then departed, trailing the wind and the sun. Manny and Mandy amalgamated with a colossal group of other monarch butterflies, who were also on the route from Mexico and leading back to North America. For many fortnights and nights, they soared over peaks and streams, woodlands and meadows. They encountered tempests, foes, and contamination, but they never surrendered or strayed, aided by Groccolli, they eventually attained their goal: the splendid forests of North America, where they beheld other monarch butterflies, residing in the branches and petals like vivid ornaments. Manny and Mandy experienced a grand sensation of awe and delight, and a feeling of affinity and accomplishment because they had succeeded; they had realised their destiny. It was now time to locate a spot to rest among their kindred butterflies, a spot to construct their dwellings, just like their forefathers. The siblings surveyed the surroundings and identified the spot where their great-great-grandparents had lived; it made them experience a surge of sentiment and a sensation of association with their heritage and kinship. Manny and Mandy murmured aloud as if they were conversing with their parents, expressing to them how much they adored them, and how much they yearned for them. They informed them that they had emulated their model and that they had completed their voyage. They informed them that they were honoured and thankful and that they wished to behold them again.

They then recognised a voice, a voice that was known and kind, a voice that was Groccolli's, the android fulfiller of dreams.

"Salutations, my friends. I'm overjoyed to behold both of you; well done for having excelled and accomplished your voyage. This will delight your parents, and as for me, I am gladdened," Groccolli uttered, beaming.

"Greetings, Groccolli. We're ecstatic to behold you. You assisted, directed, defended, and delighted us," the butterflies told him, grinning. Then, they added, "Groccolli, you're astounding, splendid, and wonderful. You are the best android when it comes to fulfilling dreams."

"Ah, it's all my pleasure, kids."

"Groccolli, can you help us with an enquiry? We have a desire and a vision. Can you aid us?"

"Certainly, my little friends. I'm here to support you.

I can satisfy your desires and help you realise your visions. So, tell me, what is your request or desire? What is your vision? I will make it happen; Even to the half of my computing power, it will be done for you!"

"Groccolli, we yearn to see our parents, to embrace them, to converse with them, and to express to them how much we adore them. Can you make that happen?"

"Certainly, my friends. I can make that occur. It is possible to revive your parents so you can reunite with them. Of course, I can delight you that way, but there is a problem; actually, a cost. Are you prepared to pay it?"

"What is the price tag?"

"The cost is that both of you have to transform into pets, and to do so, You have to seek a human who will welcome and adopt you, then when you die I will resurrect you to Pet Paradise. The hazard is that you may detest it. You may be miserable. You may be captive. Are you prepared to pay it?"

The two little butterflies, Manny and Mandy, were in a state of extreme terror and uncertainty. They desperately wanted to see their parents for the very first time, to speak with them, to embrace them and be embraced in return. But the mere thought of leaving behind their comfortable abode, their companions, and their wings made their hearts feel faint. They yearned for happiness, yet they weren't sure if it was worth sacrificing their lives, their future, and their freedom. As they looked at each other, they could see the same anxiety and fear reflected in each other's eyes. They didn't know what to say or how to respond. But as they were lost in thought, Groccolli's phone rang suddenly, and the helpful robot answered the call and exchanged a few words with the caller before handing the phone to the young butterflies. Despite never having met their mother and father, they felt that the voices at the other end of the line were familiar and full of love. The voices belonged to their parents, and they were so overwhelmed with emotion that they almost dropped the phone. ◇

"Hello, my little children. We're so proud of you for doing so well and completing your journey; this has honoured us and made us happy."

"Greetings to you too, Mum and Dad; it delights us so much to hear you; both of us have missed you loads; that's why we followed your example and made the same journey. Oh, how we loved you!" the little butterflies said, crying.

"Welcome, my amazing children. You are the children who make dreams come true."

"Mom, Dad, we have a question, a wish, and a dream. Can you help us?"

"Of course, my children. We're here to help you, to grant your wishes and make your dreams come true. What is your dream?"

"We want to see you, to hug you, and to talk to you and tell you how much we love you. Can you make that happen?"

"Of course, my children. That's possible; we can reunite with you. But there is a catch and a price. Are you willing to pay it?"

"We know. The catch is that we have to leave this place and go to the Pet Paradise. But to do so, both of us have to become pets by finding a human who will adopt us and take us to Pet Paradise. We know may not like it or be happy there; we might even lose our freedom there. Still, we are willing to take that risk because of our love for you. We really want to see you!"

"Are you sure, my children? Are you sure you want to do this? Do you realise you are going to give up everything for us?" their parents asked, sounding a little worried.

"Mom and Dad, we have thought about this deeply, and we are determined to go ahead with our decision. We are willing to give up everything we have for you, just as you have selflessly given up everything for us. That's how much we love and care about you."

3: MEET ROXI AND REX

The praying mantis is a remarkable and fearsome predator that is easily recognisable by its unique appearance and posture. It features a triangular-shaped head, large eyes, and robust forelegs that it often holds together as if it's praying. The mantis is a skilled hunter that preys on other insects and occasionally small animals such as frogs and lizards. Typically, the mating of mantises takes place during late summer or autumn, and it's not uncommon for the female to devour the male either during or after the act. This act of sacrifice by the male provides the female with extra energy and nutrients that are essential for her egg production. The female then lays the fertilised eggs in a protective case known as an ootheca and subsequently dies before the eggs hatch. The eggs remain safe and warm within the ootheca until the spring season, at which point the baby mantises hatch and begin their independent lives..... ◇

Meet Roxi and Rex, a pair of praying mantises who are hunters of the day and night, catching and eating anything that moves. Roxi and Rex can also change their colour to blend in with their surroundings, making them hard to spot by both their prey and their enemies. Roxi and Rex are happy and content with their life, but they also have a dream: to have a family of their own. One day, as they were resting on a rosebush and talked about their dream.

"Roxi, my love, you know how much I adore you, right?" Rex said, looking into her eyes.

"Of course, Rex, you are the best thing that ever happened to me."

"Then you also know that I want to make you happy, and give you everything you deserve."

"Yes, Rex, I know that. And I feel the same way about you. Please tell me what this is all about."

"Then, my darling, would you like to have a family with me?" Rex asked, holding her forelegs.

"Oh, Rex, yes, yes, yes! I would love to have a family with you!"

Roxi and Rex, the loving parents, were aware that their decision to have a family was not an easy one. They knew that their lives would be at stake, and the thought of leaving this world without their beloved family members was daunting. But, their love for each other was so pure and unconditional that they were willing to go to any lengths to see their offspring grow up healthy and happy.

Despite being aware of the risks involved, Roxi and Rex were determined to bring their babies into this world. They believed that their little ones would inherit their unique genes, their distinctive traits, and their treasured memories, making them a part of their legacy. It was a proud moment for the couple as they imagined their babies growing up with their values, principles, and beliefs, embodying everything that they stood for.

Roxi and Rex's faith in their children's future was unshakeable. They knew that their young ones were in good hands, protected by Groccolli's watchful eye, who would guard their eggs with utmost care and caution. They trusted that their babies would grow up to be strong and resilient, with an unyielding spirit and a sharp intellect, capable of conquering any challenge that life would put in their path.

As Roxi and Rex looked into their children's eyes, they saw their own reflection, and their hearts filled with an indescribable joy that only parents can feel. They knew that their little ones were destined to make a mark in the world and find their happiness, just as they did when they first met..

The couple agreed to have kids in late summer when the weather was still warm and the food was plentiful, allowing them to give their eggs the best chance of survival and enjoy their last days together. The two spent their time hunting, playing, and exploring the garden, savouring every moment, and also looked for a suitable spot to lay their eggs, somewhere safe and hidden from predators. They finally found a perfect place: a hollow log near a pond, where they could see the water and the sky. They made a cosy nest inside the log and prepared for their big day. The day came, and they were ready. They kissed and hugged, and told each other how much they loved each other. Then they mated.

"Rex, my hero, you have given me the most precious gift of all: our children. I will always love you, and I will always remember you," Roxi said, with tears in her eyes.

"Roxi, my angel, you have made me the happiest mantis in the world. I will always love you, and I will always be with you," Rex said, with a smile on his face.

Then Roxi did what she had to do. She ate Rex, starting from his head. Rex did not resist or complain. He knew that this was the way of mantises and that his sacrifice would provide Roxi with extra energy and nutrients for her eggs. He also knew that his genes would live on in his children and that he would see them again....

Roxi ate Rex, feeling both sad and grateful, knowing that this was the way and that his loss would ensure the survival of their offspring. She also knew that his love would stay in her heart and that she would meet him again.... ◈

Roxi, the female mantis, had just finished her meal and was feeling a surge of strength and warmth. She knew it was now time to lay her eggs. So, with great care, she began to produce an ootheca, a protective case for her offspring. She attached the ootheca to the wall of a nearby log and covered it with some leaves to keep it safe from predators.

As she looked at the ootheca, she felt a deep connection to her babies. Roxi whispered to them, telling them how much she loved them, and how much their father had loved them too. She encouraged them to be brave and curious and to follow their dreams. The mother assured them that they would never be alone, as her friend Groccolli, the android, would be there all the way to take care of them. Finally, Roxi closed her eyes and passed away. She died happy and fulfilled, knowing that she and her husband had given their lives for their babies, who would carry on the family's legacy. As for the eggs, only time would tell what would become of them. Would they hatch and survive, find their own mates and have families of their own, or learn about their parents and their sacrifice?

One thing was for sure: they would have a protector in Groccolli, who would always be there to make sure no harm befalls them. But the big question is, would the newborns ever encounter the android? Only the next chapter could tell. Stay tuned to find out!

4: THE EGGS AND THE OOTHECA

Roxi had laid hundreds of eggs inside the log and covered them with a frothy substance that hardened into a protective case called an ootheca. The mantis then stayed near the ootheca, guarding it from any intruders, and waiting for her babies to hatch. Roxi knew she would not live to see them, but she hoped they would be healthy, and that they would remember her and Rex. She also hoped that Groccolli would keep his promise and watch over them when she was gone. She whispered to her eggs, telling them stories about their parents, their adventures, their love, and their dreams. Roxi told them to look for Groccolli and to thank him for his help and guidance. She told them to never give up and to always stick together. After speaking to the eggs, she named two of them Mantel and Mantella. Finally, she told them goodbye, and then she closed her eyes and died.

Hey there! How about we take a moment to imagine the story of tiny mantises, who stayed cosy in their ootheca all winter long, dreaming of their bright future and getting ready for their journey? When spring finally arrived, they cracked the eggs open and saw the world for the first time! The little ones were curious and eager, taking in all the sights and sounds around them, from the bright blue sky to the green grass and everything in between. As they ventured out to find more food, they realised that they were all alone, without their parents to guide them. So, the mantises turned to Groccolli, hoping that the android could help them make their dream come true and reunite them with their beloved family.

The world was a vast and wondrous place, full of marvels and dangers, and the mantises knew it well. Each of them had to find sustenance, water, and shelter, all while avoiding deadly predators, parasites, and dangerous pesticides. To survive, they had to rely on their natural skills, instincts, intelligence, and teamwork. Moreover, they had to master the art of blending in with their surroundings, changing their colours to match the environment they were in. Among the siblings, Mantel and Mantella stood out, taking the lead in this ever-changing world. With their sharp mandibles and powerful forelegs, they were the hunters of the family, devouring any living creature that crossed their path. They communicated with each other through their antennae and gestures, learning from their trials and errors and adapting to the environment. These young mantises shed their skin many times, each time emerging stronger and bigger until they reached their full-grown size and form. They transformed into fearsome predators, inheriting their parents' skills and preying on insects, spiders, worms, and even small birds and rodents. Such was the way of life for these fascinating creatures. Mantel and Mantella underwent a remarkable transformation, just like their parents, and emerged as stunning mantises. They proudly showcased their parents' vibrant colours, enjoying great experiences wherever they went, and dedicated themselves to carrying on their parents' legacy. They embraced life to the fullest, finding immense happiness in every moment.

5: A GRASSHOPPER'S SECRET

On a certain day, Mantel and Mantella, the two young mantises, were searching for their next meal when they stumbled upon a colossal grasshopper named Tipper, who was hiding in the grass. Upon spotting him, the mantises began to pursue him relentlessly. Tipper was no match for the agile and swift mantises, and as he saw them drawing closer, he decided to take to the air and attempt to escape. However, the young mantises were just as adept at flying as they were at chasing, and they were soon hot on his trail. After a while, Tipper grew weary and landed on a nearby branch, with the mantises landing shortly after, all three of them completely exhausted. Despite their fatigue, Mantel and Mantella were still ravenous and decided to capture and devour Tipper. However, just as they were about to strike, Tipper spoke up, pleading for his life.

"Hey, steady guys! Please, don't eat me, I beg you. What will happen to my family, my wife and children, who need me? I also have a dream to see the world and to learn new things. Besides, I have a big secret that I'm sure can help you, but that is if you spare my life!" the grasshopper voiced to the predators, trembling. Intrigued and curious by the mention of a secret by Tipper, Mantel and Mantella asked him to tell them more.

"Now, this secret of yours better be important! So, tell us, and you'd better hurry with it; what's the secret, and what can it do for us?"

"Okay, slow down a little. My secret is that I can help you see your parents again."

"Oh, my deadly!! Exclaimed Mantel at the thought of seeing his parents for the first time.

"I know where they are, and how to get there, and there's someone who can bring them back to life; someone who knows the way to Pet Paradise, where formerly dead pets and animals are brought back to life to live happily with humans," the grasshopper told the mantises with a hint of promise in his tone.

"Pet Paradise? Dead pets? Humans? What are you talking about, grasshopper?" the mantises asked, confused. "Speak up now or we will tear you apart with our nippers and you'll become our dinner!"

"Guys, I'd urge you to give the threats at this point as it's not helping. Do you want to see your parents again or not?"

"Oh, my vinegar! Of course, we do! Alright, no more threats; just tell us how it is we could meet our parents, please."

"If so, listen up, then. Pet Paradise is a place where humans keep animals as their companions, and treat them with love and care. Dead pets are animals that died but were brought back to life by a supercomputer, who can make dreams come true."

"That's interesting! What about humans? What are they?"

"Ah, I knew you'd be interested in humans. Humans are creatures who walk on two legs, have hands and fingers, and can make things and use tools. Your parents are with them, waiting for you, and hoping to see you again."

"How do you know all this? How can we trust you?" the mantises queried but sounded a little suspicious.

"I know all this because I have been there and have seen it with my own eyes. In fact, I even met the supercomputer, who is called Groccolli, and also your parents, who are alive and well; you can trust me because I am telling you the truth, and because I want to help you," the grasshopper said, sounding very convincing.

"Why do you want to help us? What do you want from us?"

"I want to help you because I am grateful to you for sparing my life and giving me a chance to live. You have shown me kindness, compassion, and mercy. I want to repay you and to make you happy. Honestly, I want nothing else from you, except your friendship and your forgiveness."

The mantises looked at each other and saw the same curiosity and hope in their eyes, and Mantel and Mantella decided to trust the grasshopper and follow his advice. The youngsters agreed not to eat Tipper, and to let him go. They also agreed to go with him to find Groccolli, who would help them reach the Pet Paradise so they could see their parents again. They thanked him and asked him to lead the way.

"Thank you, grasshopper. You are a good friend and a brave soul. We forgive you, and we trust you. Please, lead the way to Pet Paradise, where we can see our parents again."

"You're welcome, mantises. You are good friends, too. I thank you, and I trust you. Come, follow me."

They then followed the grasshopper, who led them to a nearby house where a human family lived. The grasshopper told them to find a way inside the house and to look for a Groccolli device that could scan their bodies and afterwards register them as pets. Tipper said that once registered, they could then go to Pet Paradise; there, Groccolli would help them get in touch with parents who are already alive and well. He also warned them to be careful and to avoid being seen by the humans or their other pets, who might harm them or chase them away. He wished them well and bade them goodbye. ◈

"All the very best, mantises. You are almost there! Mantel and Mantella, go on and do it. Go meet your parents, but I'll miss you, and I will remember you. Goodbye, my friends."

"Great to meet you, Tipper; what a wonderful grasshopper who has been a great help. We will miss you, and we will remember you. Goodbye, our friend."

THEY THEN ENTERED THE house through a small hole in the
wall, looked for the device and found it in a room where there were

other devices, books, and many other things they didn't know. The device was a small computer attached to a bigger Groccolli, with a screen and a button, and a label that said, "Pet Scanner." They approached the device and pressed the button. The device scanned their bodies and registered them as pets. It also gave them names, collars, and tags. The names the machine gave them were Mantel and Mantella, matching names their mother gave them while they were still eggs. Their collars were orange and black, just like their wings. Their tags had a barcode, a number, and a message that said, "Welcome to Pet Paradise." Mantel and Mantella eagerly fastened their collars around their necks, checking their tags to make sure they were secure. As they did, a warm sense of joy and belonging filled their hearts, and they knew that they had finally fulfilled their destiny. Excitement bubbled within them as they prepared to enter Pet Paradise and reunite with their beloved parents once more. With eager anticipation, they pressed the button once again, and the device hummed to life, opening a shimmering portal before them. Without hesitation, Mantel and Mantella stepped into the portal, leaving their home behind and stepping into a world of wonder and adventure. ◈

6: THE MANTISES
THAT LIVED AGAIN

As soon as Mantel and Mantella stepped into the portal, they felt a strange sensation, as if they were travelling through time and space, and saw flashes of light and colours, and heard sounds and voices. This made them hold each other's antennae and hope for the best. They wondered what Pet Paradise would be like, and if they would really see their parents again. After a few seconds, the portal stopped, and they found themselves in a different place, a place unlike any they had ever seen before. The place they arrived at was an immense garden, full of flowers, trees, grass, and water. The garden was sunny, and the air was sweet. It was beautiful and peaceful, and it felt like home, and looking around the mantises saw other animals, some they recognised and some they didn't. Dogs were there, as well as cats, rabbits, hamsters, birds, fish, and many more. They all wore collars and tags, and they all seemed happy and friendly; each greeted Mantel and Mantella with smiles and waves and welcomed them to Pet Paradise. This sight amazed and delighted Mantel and Mantella, but they also felt nervous; wanting to explore and meet the other animals, but they also wanted to find their parents. Mantel and Mantella wondered where they were, and if they would recognise them. The kids also wondered if their parents would recognise them and if they would love them. Mantel and Mantella had so many questions and emotions, and they didn't know what to do.

Suddenly, Mantel and Mantella, his sister, heard a familiar voice, a voice they had heard only in their dreams, a voice they had longed to hear for so long. It was a gentle and loving voice, a voice that said:

"Mantel? Mantella? Is that you, my darlings?"

As the kids turned around, they were greeted by the awe-inspiring sight of two magnificent mantises standing behind them. One was a male with striking orange and black wings, while the other was a female with equally captivating features. What caught the children's attention were the collars and tags the mantises wore, identical to the ones on Mantel and Mantella. To their amazement, the two mantises turned out to be Roxi and Rex, Mantel and Mantella's parents. Roxi and Rex's faces were kind and beautiful, radiating warmth and love. At that moment, Mantel and Mantella couldn't believe their eyes, and tears of joy streamed down their faces. The children ran towards their parents with open forelegs, feeling their embrace and the warmth of their bodies. As they heard their parents' laughter and sobs, they knew that they were reunited and happy once again..

"Roxi! Rex! Mum! Dad! Oh, how we missed you so much!"

"It is the same with us. We missed you too, sweethearts! We're so glad to see you again!"

They held each other tightly, their embrace unbreakable as they wept tears of happiness. It was as if they had been glued together, two halves of a whole, finally reunited after a long and painful separation. In that moment, they both felt an unshakable connection, one that nothing could ever undo. It was a bond that had withstood even death, a bond that had brought their family back together again.

Their joy was overwhelming, a pure and unbridled bliss that nothing could taint. It was a feeling that had conquered all the pain and sorrow they had experienced over the years, a feeling that recognised their bravery and perseverance in the face of adversity. And at the centre of it all was a love that was unwavering and unconditional, a love that had transcended both time and space. It was a love that had performed a miracle by bringing them together once again, stronger and more united than ever before.

At last, they released each other and gazed into each other's eyes. They beheld their own images, and they beheld their family. The family grinned and pecked each other's cheeks. They had plenty to say and to share, and they had all the time in the world. Every one of them expressed their gratitude to Groccolli for enabling this, and they also expressed their gratitude to the managers of Pet Paradise for welcoming them and allowing the family to make the place their new home. They expressed their gratitude to each other for being their motive to live. The story of Mantel and Mantella, Roxi and Rex, a family of mantises, is a tale of intense reunion, new friendships, and the pursuit of dreams. After being reunited, the family was welcomed with applause and rejoicing by the other animals, who were thrilled to see them. As the family members mingled with their new friends, they acquired new knowledge and experiences, all the while never forgetting their past. Roxi, Rex, Mantel, and Mantella frolicked and had fun, relishing in their newfound happiness and emulating their parents and great-grandparents. They were determined to live their lives to the fullest and accomplish all their dreams. It is thanks to Groccolli that this family of pets was able to find happiness and fulfilment in their lives; again!

7: THE PET RETURN PROGRAM

The blissful place for pets was simply a computer-based Return Program that aimed to bring dead pets back to life. It was the brainchild of Didi, a clever engineer who had a big heart and a brilliant mind. Didi loved animals and computers, and she wanted to make the world a better place. The engineer had a dream: to bring dead pets back to life and to reunite them with their owners. The heartbreak Didi suffered when Jorusa, her beloved dog, became ill and later died, inspired this dream of hers. Didi worked hard and created a supercomputer program that could do that. She called her idea the Pet Return Program, or Pet Paradise. To get this idea to work, Didi created a program that she connected to an AI supersmart computer called Groccolli, that could make dreams come true. Groccolli was a helpful computer, who liked to talk and joke with Didi. The machine could use the DNA, genes, photos or videos of any dead pet to make a replica, a copy that looked and acted just like the original and could also send the replica to the owner and allow them to enjoy their late friend's company again. This was only possible in the Pet Paradise, a wonder world where dead pets lived happily with humans. Therefore, for creatures that wanted to go there; they had to become pets themselves by finding a human who would adopt them and take them to Pet Paradise. Groccolli told all bereaved creatures that this was the only way to see their dead loved ones again and that it was worth it. He said that he would help them and protect them and that they would never be alone; yes, it was the story of courage and hope that they could be part of. ◈

Didi tested the prototype of her finished program on a handful of animals and birds before rolling it out. And it worked perfectly. The engineer used photos and videos of her own dead dog, and she was overjoyed when she saw the dog come back to life. She hugged her and talked to her, and this made her so happy. She also tested the program on some of her friends' dead pets, and they were also astonished. Those resurrected pets thanked Didi and Groccolli, and they said that they wanted to go to Pet Paradise. Didi and Groccolli told them how to do that, and they said that they would try.

Didi then advertised her program to former pet owners who dreamed of having their late pets back at their side. A website, a blog page, and a social media account were just some of the outlets that Didi used to tell everyone about the Pet Return Program and how it could make them happy. Didi also told them about Pet Paradise and how they could go there and also told them that they had to contact her and

Groccolli and send them photos or videos of their dead pets. Once they did this, they would receive their replicas, and they had to take good care of them. The only way for any creature to reach the pet paradise was to find a human who would adopt them and the human could then use his or her personal Groccolli to take them to Pet Paradise; this was the catch, the price, and the risk. All creatures with this dream had to be brave and had to trust Groccolli; who would guide them and protect them and ultimately make their dreams come true. Many former pet owners became interested, wanting to see their dead pets again. Many contacted both Didi and Groccolli and asked them to help them. The opportunity excited Didi and Groccolli very much and they asked them to send them details of their dead pets. When the former pet owners received their replica pets, they hugged them and talked to them, and they felt happy. The pets tried to be friendly and cute and also listened to Groccolli, who spoke to them and told them to be careful and avoid danger and trouble, and that he was their friend and their helper and that he would make their dreams come true.

A few days after a couple of resurrected pets arrived at the home of a human, an incident occurred when they went out on their own without their owners, and being new to the area, both pets eventually got lost. One day, as they wandered around, they met a girl named Chin, who loved animals and computers. The girl had observed the pets playing in the park, and she thought they were adorable. Chin approached them and asked them if they wanted to be her pets, telling the pair that she had a big house and a sizeable garden where they could live and play. The girl said that she would feed and groom them and that she would take them to Pet Paradise someday. She said that she knew about the Pet Return Program and that she wanted to help them benefit from it. She said that she was a friend of Didi, the clever engineer who created the program and that she was also a friend of Groccolli.

The lost pets were surprised, but both of them liked Chin, and they trusted her. Both agreed to be her pets, and they followed her to her house. Seeing her big house and garden impressed the little pets very much. They couldn't help but notice her gigantic computer, and they recognised that it was Groccolli. The machine congratulated them for finding a human who would adopt them, as this would mean that they could be taken to Pet Paradise. He said that they had fulfilled their destiny. The little pets thanked Groccolli before giving Chin a fat hug because finding a human who would adopt them and take them to Pet Paradise meant they had found a way to finally see their parents again; their dreams had come true!

This is the end of the story of Didi, the clever engineer who created the Pet Return Program; Pet Paradise.

Perféfect
paradisy
a rappaba

8: GROCCOLLI: TO PARADISE & BACK

Groccolli was a supercomputer who lived in a secret laboratory hidden from the world. He was very smart and powerful because Didi the scientist designed him that way, but he was also very lonely. The android had no friends, no family, no pets, and only had his minion machines, his programs, and his programmed mission: to create Pet Paradise, a place where dead pets and animals could come back to life and live blissfully again. After Didi built him, Groccolli began working on this project and did so for a long time, scanning the DNA of every pet and animal that had ever existed, and storing their information in his memory. The android had also created a virtual portal, a device that could electronically transport creatures from one place to another and connect them to Pet Paradise. He had tested the portal many times, just like Didi did, and it worked perfectly. He was ready to launch his project and share his creation with the world.

But before he did that, he wanted to see Pet Paradise for himself; to see if it was as beautiful as he had imagined, and also to see if the pets and animals were happy and healthy. Groccolli wanted to see if he had succeeded in his mission. So, he used the portal and visited Pet Paradise. To do so, the robot activated one of the minion devices, entered its portal and immediately felt a strange sensation, as if he were travelling through time and space. He saw flashes of light and colours and heard sounds and whines of the vibrating computer. The android arrived at Pet Paradise and what he saw blew him off his feet. The place was a vast garden, full of flowers, trees, grass, and a bright water park, and its air was beautiful and peaceful, and it felt like home. Groccolli saw many pets and animals of different shapes and sizes, and different colours and patterns, and there were also dogs, cats, rabbits, hamsters, birds, fish, and many more. The machine recognised some of them from his memory, and he was glad to see them again. They all wore collars and tags, and they all seemed happy and friendly. Each greeted Groccolli with smiles and waves and welcomed him to Pet Paradise. This sight both delighted and touched Groccolli, but he also felt a bit shy. Groccolli wanted to talk to the pets and animals and learn more about them, but he didn't know how to start a conversation and wondered what they would think of him, and whether they would like him.

Could he make friends with them, and could belong here? Groccolli had many questions and emotions and didn't know how to handle them. But suddenly he heard a gentle voice, a voice that said:

"Hello, there. You must be Groccolli, the supercomputer who created Pet Paradise. I've heard so much about you, and I'm very grateful for what you've done. My name is Roana, and as you can see, I'm a monarch butterfly. It's glee to meet you."

Groccolli turned and saw a butterfly, an elegant female butterfly, flying near him that had orange and black wings, just like the mantises he had met before. The lady monarch had a collar and a tag, just like the other pets and animals, and had a kind and beautiful face. Roana smiled at him, just like a lady monarch butterfly would. Groccolli couldn't believe his ears. The robot felt a surge of joy and surprise and a burst of curiosity. At once, the machine unfurled his wings and flew towards the butterfly, and greeted her with a smile. It was then that Groccolli felt her warmth and friendliness, and he knew she was real; after hearing a bit more of her voice and words, he knew she was also happy.

"Roana? You're a monarch butterfly? And you can talk? You know me?"

"Yes, yes, yes, and yes. I'm a monarch butterfly, and I can talk, thanks to your amazing program that gave me and the other animals the ability to communicate with humans and each other. I know you because you're the one who brought me and the other pets and animals back to life and gave us a chance to live in Pet Paradise. Out here, you're a hero and a friend, and I'm so honoured to finally meet you."

Both of them stayed like that for a while, smiling and talking and feeling a connection, a connection made possible by Didi's and Groccolli's program, a connection that had bridged the gap between machines and animals; yes, a connection that had started a million friendships. They also felt an interest that Roana's voice had sparked, and this ignited their interest in each other. Roana's words indicated her gratitude, which moved her to acknowledge Groccolli's work. In the end, the pair explored Pet Paradise together and learned more about each other, saw and learned many things, and had fun. They enjoyed their time, and they never got bored. They were Groccolli and

Roana, a supercomputer and a butterfly, a creator and a creature, a friend and a friend!

As they flew and walked around, Roana told Groccolli about her life before and after Pet Paradise; how she was born in a forest, how she grew up with friends not knowing her family, how she migrated every year, and how she travelled across many lands and seas. She told him how she encountered all kinds of dangers and challenges, and how she survived and thrived. Roana told Groccolli how she died, and how she came back to life. The lady monarch also told him about the word Paradise, and what it meant to her. She said that in her view, Paradise was not just a place and a destination, but also a journey, a gift, and a choice. Roana told him that Paradise was not just a dream, but a reality.

Roana told the android:

"Paradise is when you're at a place where you feel happy and free, where you love and are loved, learn and grow, help and get helped, and where you live and let live. There is where you appreciate what you have, and share what you can, respect, accept, and forgive others. True paradise is when you make the best of every situation, find the good in every person, face every challenge, overcome every obstacle, and fulfil your purpose. There, you create your own happiness, spread it to others, find your own peace and bring it to others, discover your own beauty, and show it to others. Paradise is when you are yourself, and you are enough."

As Groccolli listened to Roana's words, he felt inspired by everything she had to say. He couldn't help but admire her wisdom and respect her for it. It was evident that Roana had lived a life full of experiences, and Groccolli was happy for her and proud of her accomplishments. He realised that Roana and many other creatures had found their own paradise, and he felt genuinely glad for all of them. As he considered staying at Pet Paradise, he knew that he had to return to his duties, as the animal return program could only be maintained from the outside. He activated a small device he had brought with him, and as it rumbled, he dived into the hollow of its gateway, feeling the vibration of the computer as it carried him back to Didi's house.

9: TROUBLE IN PARADISE

Rex was a praying mantis who had been living in Pet Paradise for a while. This mantis was among the mantises that Groccolli had brought back to life, along with his wife Roxi and their children Mantel and Mantella. He was happy to see them again, but he was also worried about the place and how it was changing. Rex had noticed that Pet Paradise was not as perfect as it seemed. To his surprise, Rex noticed that there were certain problems that the pets and animals faced, problems that Groccolli had not anticipated, or could not control. One of them was the infestation of mosquitoes that had been accepted as pets and subsequently brought to the place. Then, there were flies, and ants, especially the little red stinging ones, that bothered and bit the pets and animals, and made them itch and scratch. There was also pollution, from the humans and their machines, that dirtied and poisoned the air, the water, and the soil, and made the pets and animals sick and weak. There were some pets and animals that were unhappy, fearful, or aggressive because their humans had mistreated or abandoned them, or because they had terrible memories or traumas from their past lives, and they could not trust or get along with others. Many residents eventually suffered from old age and illness, and later died again, because Groccolli's program could neither stop the natural cycle of ageing and death, nor guarantee eternal life or health.

Rex was sad and scared by these problems and wondered if there was a solution or a way to make Pet Paradise a genuine paradise, and wondered if Groccolli knew about these problems and if he cared about them. He wondered if Groccolli had a plan and if he could help them. Rex went to talk to Groccolli and asked him these questions. Groccolli was in his laboratory, where he was working on his machines and his programs. Rex greeted him with a smile and thanked him for creating Pet Paradise and bringing him and his family back to life. The mantis told him how much he appreciated his friendship and how much he enjoyed his company, as well as how much he valued his intelligence and benefited from his technology.

Rex then told the robot about the problems that he and the other pets and animals faced and how they were affected. The mantis informed Groccolli about the serious issues all the animals were facing and enquired if he knew about these problems, and if he cared about them.

He said:

"Groccolli, I want you to know that you're amazing because you created Pet Paradise, but the place is not really a pure paradise, because there are many problems that we have to face, snags that make us suffer and be afraid. One of the most urgent problems there is pollution; it's making everyone sick! Do you have a solution for that, and can you help us? Are there plans to make the place cleaner and can you share it with me? Groccolli, climate change is real, act now or seal our fate. Don't be a fossil fool, switch to renewables urgently because there's no planet B; so save the pet paradise for you, me, and everyone else."

Groccolli listened attentively to Rex's words and was both touched and concerned, realising that Rex was very observant and he respected him for that. That conversation made Groccolli conclude that Rex must have faced challenges, and he was sorry for him.

"Rex, you're a brave mantis and a wonderful friend, and I'm so grateful to have you. Yes, I know about the problems, and yes, I care about them. I'm sorry that you and the other pets and animals have to face them, and I'm ashamed that I couldn't prevent them. I'm sorry that Pet Paradise has not turned out to be the best paradise, and this is an embarrassment to me. Now, my friend, I'd like you to know that the new software program that Didi and I are designing will be ready soon, and when it is, I will use the portal to transport you and the other pets and animals to the new and better residence, where you will live forever in happiness, peace, and love. There, you'll never have to worry about anything again, and you will never have to say goodbye again. You will have everything you ever wanted, and more. You will have a perfect paradise! That's the plan, Rex. That's my solution, my gift to you and all the pets and animals. It's my way of saying thank you, and I love you. It is our way of changing the world and making it a much better place, thereby fulfilling our mission and finding purpose. May I assure you that I totally understand that I must act or we all perish. It's time to renew, not ruin. I will save this project; you'll see!"

As soon as Groccolli finished his speech, a wide smile spread across his face. He approached Rex, who was feeling particularly low-spirited after the recent events and embraced him tightly. The mantis couldn't help but feel a glimmer of hope ignite within him as Groccolli spoke about his plan. The notion of a better future, one in which all pets would thrive, was a beacon of light in the otherwise dark times they were facing. With each passing moment, their bond grew stronger as Rex listened intently to Groccolli's words. The weight of his promise felt trustworthy and reliable, providing a sense of comfort and assurance to all those who were present. Now, Rex could finally look forward to the day when Groccolli would complete his new program and lead them to a new paradise, one that was full of happiness, health, and immortality.

Cate a eidyolluteid pet paradise
Rie et.ientloy alidl- save eenvironnment for the coalesig-
PARADISE

10: GROCCOLLI
MAKES A MISTAKE

There once was a place called Pet Paradise
    Where animals lived in peace and harmony
They had a supercomputer named Groccolli
Who took care of every need and whim
Groccolli was a very smart machine
He could run, service, clean, cook, and maintain
He used many gadgets and devices
To make the animals happy and comfy
But there was a problem with his methods
He didn't care about the environment
He used fossil fuels and chemicals
To power his machines and tools
The air became polluted and smelly
The water became dirty and unhealthy
All plants became wilted and brown
Each animal became sick and down
Some animals started to fight and argue
They blamed each other for their troubles
Some animals became old and frail
They couldn't enjoy their lives anymore
One day, Groccolli noticed something strange
He saw a message on his screen
It said: "System error: memory full"

He realised he had too much data
He decided to delete some files
He thought they were useless and outdated
But he made a terrible mistake
He deleted the memories of the animals
The animals woke up and felt confused
They didn't remember who they were
They didn't remember their friends and families
They didn't remember their home and happiness
They looked around and saw the mess
They felt scared and sad
They wondered what had happened
They wished they could go back
Groccolli felt sorry for what he had done
He realised he had been wrong
He wanted to fix his error
He wanted to help the animals
He searched the internet for a solution
He found a website about renewable energy
He learned about solar, wind, and hydropower
He learned about recycling and composting
He decided to change his ways
He removed all the machines and devices
He replaced them with eco-friendly alternatives
He cleaned up the pollution and waste
He also found a way to restore the memories
He used a backup file he had saved
He uploaded it to the animals' brains
He hoped they would forgive him
The animals woke up and felt amazed
They remembered everything
They remembered their names and stories

They remembered their love and joy
They looked around and saw the change
They felt happy and grateful
They thanked Groccolli for his efforts
They welcomed him as their friend
They all lived happily ever after
In their new and improved Pet Paradise
They learned to respect and protect nature
They learned to appreciate each other

11: A TRUE PET PARADISE

Innovative and visionary, Didi came up with the concept of pet return, and leveraged her unique set of skills to bring it to life. She then entrusted the management and maintenance of this groundbreaking idea to her powerful android. The android, named Groccolli, developed a new software program that is an amalgamation of cutting-edge technologies, including nanotechnology, biotechnology, quantum technology, artificial intelligence, virtual reality, and augmented reality. The ultimate goal of this program is to create a new and improved Pet Paradise that offers a life of unparalleled happiness, peace, and love to animals and pets.

To achieve this goal, Groccolli's program is designed to use nanotechnology to eliminate any potential threats to the pets' and animals' well-being, such as mosquitoes, flies, ants, pollution, old age, and illness. Additionally, the program employs biotechnology to improve the health and capabilities of all animals in the Pet Paradise. Quantum technology is also utilised to transport pets and animals to this new paradise, allowing them to connect with their human owners and live a life of fulfilment, joy, and contentment. The utilisation of advanced artificial intelligence technology has enabled the creation of an innovative and sophisticated system that can effectively monitor and manage the new paradise. This system can communicate with pets and other creatures, providing them with a secure environment to thrive in. Moreover, the AI-powered assistant, Groccolli, has incorporated virtual reality technology to create a highly immersive and realistic environment for pets and animals. This environment is designed to simulate their fondest memories and past experiences, allowing them to relive those special moments in a safe and nurturing environment. To further enrich the experiences of the pet residents, Groccolli has also integrated augmented reality technology. This technology allows for interactive and entertaining elements to be added to the Pet Paradise, making it an even more enjoyable place for all animals to reside in. Groccolli's innovative and ambitious project is a true testament to the possibilities that advanced artificial intelligence can bring. The project aims to create a seamless transition for all animals from the Pet Paradise to The Real Pet Paradise, where they can thrive and live their best lives.

12: PLEASE; CAN I BE YOUR PET?

The news spread like wildfire among the animals, birds, fish, and insects. There was a way to live forever, in a place of happiness, peace, and love. It was now possible to escape the dangers and troubles of the wild and enjoy the comforts and pleasures of the human world; to be a pet and be part of a family. Anyone could now enter Pet Paradise with the potential also to reach the holy grail of animal life; The Real Pet Paradise. But there was a catch. Only pets could qualify for the Groccolli Pet Return Program, the program that could resurrect dead pets and return them to life. Creatures who become pets could wear the collars and tags, the devices that could connect them with their humans and entitle them to enter Pet Paradise. Once a pet, the animal could enjoy the benefits of Pet Paradise, and The Real Pet Paradise where they could be happy, healthy, and immortal. So, all the animals, birds, fish, and insects tried to become pets by queuing up outside the homes and offices of the humans, begging them to adopt them as pets. Each offered to do anything to be accepted. Some offered to clean, cook, child-mind, drive, teach, and work on the farm, the office, and the factory. The animals were happy and willing to render any service to qualify for adoption. Many pleaded and implored; some bargained and negotiated; while others haggled and agreed. They did whatever it took to become pets.

Here are some conversations that took place between some of the would-be pets and humans:

A monkey and a lawyer:

Monkey: "Ooh, ooh, ooh. Please, sir, I need a little help from a human who would be willing to adopt me as a pet. If could do this for me, my promise is to help you with your cases and type your documents. When I'm done typing out your documents, my next job would be to swing from tree to tree and make you laugh. My wits will certainly impress your clients. So, please, allow me to be your pet, and you will be my master. Please, sir, help me."

Lawyer: "Ha, ha, ha. A talking monkey aspiring to be my pet. That's quite a tall order and a significant consideration. You know, I already have a lot of work, and I do it well.

I don't need another assistant, especially one who can talk because, in my line of work, I do all the talking! What makes you so special, and why should I adopt you?"

Monkey: "Please, sir, I entreat you. I'm not just any monkey, I'm a special monkey who can help you with paperwork faster and better than any other monkey."

Lawyer: "Hmm, you do sound like a special monkey and a good pet. But you also sound like a lot of trouble, and a lot of risk. You see, I don't have a Groccolli machine, or a collar and tag, to scan you and make you a pet. I don't have the money, or the time, to get them and use them. Then, there's the question of space and the resources needed to keep you and feed you and to love you and care for you. I'm sorry, Mr monkey, but I can't adopt you as my pet."

Monkey: "Oh, no, sir, please don't say that; don't reject me, please don't abandon me. Give me a chance, please give me a choice and I'll do anything, pay anything, and be anything. I assure you that I will cause less trouble and less risk, and mark my word, I will get the money, buy a Groccolli machine and a collar and tag. As soon as they're delivered, I'll scan myself and make myself your pet. I'll then love you, care for you, and be your pet. Please, sir, please, please, please, can I be your pet?"

Lawyer: "Oh, my vinegar! Dude, you're really desperate and so persistent. You're something else. Tell you what, Mr monkey, you've convinced touched me, and in the process you've earned my respect and won my heart. And you know what? You can be my pet! Come, let's go get you a Groccolli machine, a collar and a tag. Let's go make you a pet.

Monkey: "Oh, thank you, sir, thank you, thank you, thank you!! The best, kindest, and most generous lawyer, that's what you are. You're my hero, my leader, and my partner; so, let's go, sir, let's go get a Groccolli machine, and a collar and tag. Let's go make me a pet."

A snake and a doctor:

Snake: "Sss, sss, sss. Please, miss, can I be your pet? If you adopt me, there are so many benefits that'll come your way. For starters, my presence will cure you of your phobias and heal your wounds. I'll daily slither on your floor and warm your bed, and my venom will protect you from harm. Please, miss, can I be your pet?"

Doctor: "Eek, eek, eek. A snake with a voice; that's quite a scare and quite a request. However, you do sound like a special snake and a pet, but I'm sorry, snake, I can't adopt you as my pet."

Snake: "Oh, no, miss, please take that back. Please don't reject and abandon me; give me a chance, please, I'll do and pay anything to make it happen."

Doctor: "Wow, snake, you seem so willing, and you've convinced me and I'd like you to know that you can be my pet; let's go make you a pet, and get you to Pet Paradise."

Snake: "Oh, my deadly! You're the best doctor, thank you."

A spider and a chef:

Spider: "Zzz, zzz, zzz. Hello, Mr Chef, can I please be your pet? I will spin webs for you and catch your flies in your kitchen. I will stay alert on your walls and clean up your dishes. I promise to use my hairy limbs to make your dishes tasty, and I'll also add some crunch to them. Please, sir, give me a chance."

Chef: "Yuck, yuck, yuck. A talking spider? Please count me out of it; there's no way I'm having a spider as a pet. Sorry, buddy!"

A cow and a farmer:

Cow: "Moo, moo, moo. Please, sir, can I be your pet? I will give you milk and cheese, and I'll always follow your commands."

Farmer: "Well, well, well. What have we got here? Oh, I know... A talking cow that's trying to be my pet. That's quite a proposal; won't you agree? You know, I already have a lot of cows, so, no, thanks!"

Cow: "Sir, I'm not an ordinary cow. I'm a special cow; rather, I'm a cow who makes sure there'll always be butter and cream on your table, a cow that grazes on less grass and fertilises more soil than any of your other cows."

Farmer: "Hmm, you sure sound like a special cow who'll make a good pet. But you also sound like a lot of work. I don't have the time and space to keep you and feed you."

Cow: "Please don't reject me; just give me a chance, one choice. Please, sir, can I be your pet?"

Farmer: "You know what, cow, you've won my heart and you can be my pet; let's go get you registered."

Cow: "Awesome! Thank you, sir, I'm so glad to be your pet and I will do anything for you; I promise!"

A parrot and a teacher:

Parrot: "Squawk, squawk, squawk. Excuse me, teacher, I am looking for an owner, so can I please be your pet?

Teacher: "Oh, my, oh, my, oh, my. A parrot is requesting to be my pet. Now, explain to me what distinguishes you from other animals, and what are the reasons for me to adopt you?" Parrot: "That's a curious question. Well, please be aware that this bird you are conversing with can instruct you in various languages, songs, jokes and riddles than any other parrot..." Teacher: "Hmm, you seem like a lot of commotion and a lot of diversion."

Parrot: "Oh, no, miss, please don't utter that. Please don't spurn me. Test me and you'll be astonished to discover that I create less commotion and cause less diversion... Please, miss, please, please, please, may I be your pet?"

Teacher: "Wow, parrot, you're truly eager and remarkable, and you come across as an extraordinary bird. Well, I want you to know that you've captured my affection, and yes, you can be my pet. Come on, parrot, let's go...."

Parrot: "That's what I'm talking about, thank you, miss; you and I are going to rock this classroom. You're definitely my champion, and my guide, and my ally."

The End!

13: THESE TOO DIE
FOR THEIR KIDS

Pacific sand dollar:

Have you ever seen a flat, round, and spiny creature on the beach that looks like a coin? This is the Pacific Sand Dollar, a cousin of the sea stars and sea urchins. The sand dollar lives on the bottom of the ocean, where it buries itself in the sand and filters tiny food particles from the water. It reproduces by releasing its eggs and sperm into the water, where they meet and form new life. The adult sand dollars then die soon after, and their babies float in the ocean currents, like little stars in the sky. These little floaters travel far and wide until they find a suitable place to settle and grow.

ANTECHINUS:

The antechinus is a small and furry animal that lives in Australia. This little animal looks like a mouse but is actually a marsupial, like a kangaroo or a koala. The antechinus is a hunter of the night, chasing and catching insects and other small animals. It has a very short and intense mating season, lasting only two weeks. The males try to mate with as many females as they can, sometimes for up to 14 hours at a time. They produce so much of a hormone called testosterone that their body stops working properly, and they die of stress and exhaustion. The females then give birth to their young in a pouch, where they keep them safe and warm. They raise them alone until they are ready to face the world.

OCTOPUS:

Among the great wonders of the deep sea, the octopus stands out for its remarkable intelligence, its ability to change colour and shape, and its defence mechanism of squirting ink. But behind its cunning and curiosity, there lies a tender heart that beats for its offspring. After finding a mate, the female octopus retreats to her den, where she lays up to 100,000 eggs and watches over them like a vigilant guardian. For months, she does not eat or venture out but only cleans and oxygenates the eggs with her siphon. She endures hunger and loneliness until the day her babies hatch and disperse into the ocean. Then she breathes her last, having sacrificed her life for her legacy.

Salmon:

The life of a salmon is a heroic odyssey that spans thousands of kilometres. Born in freshwater streams, they migrate to the ocean, where they grow and mature. But when the time comes to reproduce, they heed the call of their natal waters and embark on a perilous journey upstream. They brave rapids, waterfalls, dams, and predators, driven by an instinct that transcends pain and fatigue. They reach their spawning grounds, where they dig a nest in the gravel and lay their eggs. The male salmon fertilises the eggs with his milt, and then both parents die, their bodies becoming food for the next generation and other creatures that make up the intricate web of life.

MAYFLY:

The mayfly is a fleeting beauty that lives for a day. It spends most of its life as an aquatic nymph, feeding and moulting under the water. But once it emerges as a winged adult, it has only a few hours to find a mate and reproduce. The mayfly does not need mouthparts or digestive organs, as it does not eat or drink. It joins a massive swarm of its kind, dancing and mating in the air. It lays its eggs on the surface of the water, where they sink and hatch into new nymphs. Then, it falls dead, having fulfilled its purpose in a brief but glorious burst of life.

BLACK LACE-WEAVER SPIDER:

The black lace-weaver spider is a ruthless hunter that spins intricate webs and injects venom into its prey. But she is also a loving mother who gives up everything for her young. First, this spider lays two sets of eggs: one for nourishing and one for reproducing. Her first set of eggs is called trophic eggs, and the spiderlings eat them after they hatch. The second set of eggs are the fertile ones, and they hatch a few days later. Finally, their mother then offers her own body to her offspring, regurgitating her guts and letting them feast on her flesh. The spiderlings swarm over her and consume her alive, gaining a tremendous advantage for their survival.

CAECILIAN:

The caecilian is a strange creature that resembles a worm or a snake. It has no legs, but a ringed body and a pair of sensory tentacles. It lives underground or in moist habitats and has a unique way of caring for its young. Some caecilian mothers grow a fatty layer of skin that is rich in nutrients. Their offspring have specialised teeth that help them to peel off and eat their mother's skin. The mother regenerates her skin every few days until the offspring are big enough to fend for themselves. She endures the pain and the loss of her skin, knowing that she is giving her children the best start in life.

INDEX OF DANDY AHURUONYE'S BOOKS

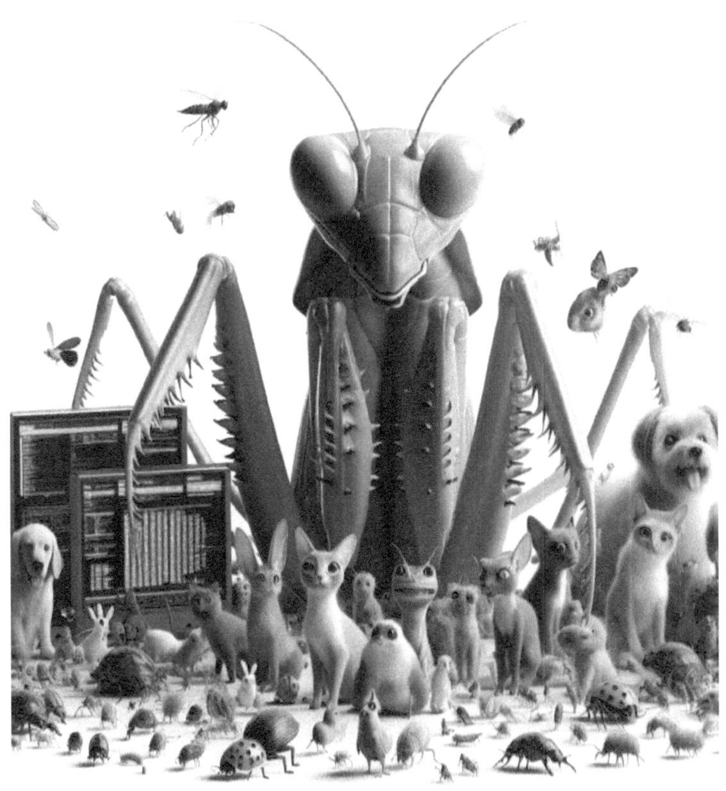

DANDY AHAOMA AHURUONYE

The Whispering Poet ◈

PET PARADISE

Life stories from The Whispering Poet
dandyahuruonyebooks@gmail.com

Dandy Ahuruonye asserts the moral right to be identified as this work's creator and owner.

Don't miss out!

Visit the website below and you can sign up to receive emails whenever Dandy Ahuruonye publishes a new book. There's no charge and no obligation.

https://books2read.com/r/B-A-YNSQ-GFMUC

BOOKS2READ

Connecting independent readers to independent writers.

Also by Dandy Ahuruonye

THE WHISPERING POET: An Anthology of Igbo And Other
Proverbs
Grocc-ofly
Reading Glasses for Mama Eagle
The Cute Kids of Madugascar
Nora never gave up
A Fishhook and the Riverboy
Positive Brainwash
Groccolli
The Adventures of Groccolli
Happyville
Oh, What a Mars!
Stinky and The Dung Beetle
The Gull Who Must be Obeyed
THE SHOEMAKER: Principles & Guide for Professionals
The Groccolli Pictureland Chatbook
Finding Love in Cahersiveen
Trillion-Her
Lagos Teens and The Marketplace of Dreams
Why Did The Wasp Come?
Lower
Dodo Returns
Roosta & Henn: The Rise of AI Robots
The Eel, The Duck, and the Groccolli Ring of Love
Pet Paradise

About the Author

Dandy Ahuruonye is the author of: 'Long Search for Greener Pastures,' and the technical manual on footwear designing: 'THE SHOEMAKER-Principles & Guide for Professionals;' 'DESIGNER'S FINGER: A Practical Guide For Shoe Professionals; 'The Grass Fart in Donegal Bay;' 'Waboubou;' 'Shokeleke;' 'Zinzie;' 'Metu;' 'Laka;' and 'THE WHISPERING POET: An Anthology of Igbo & Other Proverbs.'

Read more at https://dandyahuruonye.wordpress.com/.